The Singer

D1086518

ALSO BY BARBARA HURD

Entering the Stone: On Caves and Feeling Through the Dark

Stirring the Mud: On Swamps, Bogs, and Human Imagination

The Singer's Temple

Poems
Barbara Hurd

Bright Hill Press
Treadwell, New York
2003

iv

THE SINGER'S TEMPLE

POEMS

BARBARA HURD

Book and cover design: Bertha Rogers
Cover art: "Garden Room" watercolor on paper
Author's Photograph: Photography by Jeannine

Editor in Chief: Bertha Rogers
Editorial Staff: Earl W. Roberts III; Ernest M. Fishman,
　　　　　　　Margot Farrington
Copyright 2003 © by Barbara Hurd

Library of Congress Cataloguing-in-Publication Data

Hurd, Barbara
　The singer's temple : poems / by Barbara Hurd.
　　p. cm. -- (Bright Hill Press poetry book award series ; no. 7)
　ISBN 1-892471-20-5 (alk. paper)
　1. Twins--Poetry. 2. Difference (Psychology)--Poetry. I. Title. II
Series.

　PS3608.U766S56 2003
　811'.6--dc22
　　　　　　　　　　　　　　　2003019089
The Singer's Temple
is published by Bright Hill Press.
Bright Hill Press, Inc., a not-for-profit, 501(c)(3) literary and educational organiza-
tion, was founded in 1992. The organization is registered with the New York State
Department of State, Office of Charities Registration. Publication of *The Singer's
Temple* is made possible, in part, with public funds from the Literature Program of the
New York State Council on the Arts, a State agency.

Editorial Address:
Bright Hill Press, Inc.
POB 193, 94 Church Street
Treadwell, NY 13846-0193
Voice: 607-829-5055
Fax: 607-829-5056
E-Mail: wordthur@stny.rr.com
Web Site: www.brighthillpress.org

NYSCA

All rights reserved. Except for brief quotation in critical articles or reviews, this book,
or parts thereof, must not be reproduced in any form or by any means, electronic or
mechanical, including photocopy, recording, or any information storage and retrieval
system, without permission in writing from the publisher. Requests for permission to
make copies of any part of the work should be mailed to Bright Hill Press, POB 193,
94 Church Street, Treadwell, NY 13846-0193.

ACKNOWLEDGMENTS

Grateful acknowledgment is made to the following publications for poems that originally appeared in them:

Earlier versions of "Negative Capability," "After Listening to the Surviving Siamese Twin," "First Supper," "At the Manger," "One Here, One There," and "Let There be Peace" were first published by Artscape in a limited edition chapbook entitled *Objects in This Mirror*; "Fireflies" and "Sudden Exposure," *Antietam Review*; "Motorcycle Riding with a Sadhu" and "What Precedes," *Connecticut Review*; "Molting" and "To the Grackle Who Fell Down the Stove Pipe in a Blizzard," *Convolvulus*; "Peter Pan," *Earth's Daughters*; "On Hearing His Daughter Try to Play Offenbach's Tales of Hoffman" and "Twinleaf," *Heliotrope*; "Doubting Thomas," *New Letters*; "Long-Term Pregnancy" and "Great Egret," *Nimrod*; "Caving Without the Shaman," *Outerbridge*; " "Longing," *Painted Bride*; and "Russian Water Grandfather," *Prairie Schooner*.

For Ann and Kenny

A god can do it. But tell me, how can a man
follow his narrow road through the strings?
A man is split. And where two roads intersect
inside us, no one has built the Singer's Temple.

Rilke
(tr. Robert Bly)

CONTENTS

ONE

I am not I
I am this one
walking beside you whom I do not see.
—Juan Ramon Jimenez

DISQUIET

And twofold always—May God us keep
From Single Vision & Newton's sleep.
—William Blake

Sixteen, and already
every voice inside me
had its opposite, its dissenter,
a *yes*, but for every *therefore*,

the counter responses
canceling each other out
in the adolescent urge
not to look stupid,

a silence in the classroom
even the teacher who knew
my great love of Blake
tried to warn me about.

Years later at an all night party
I didn't say a single word
and a woman said about me,
still waters run deep.

I thought her a fool
and loved her admiration,
I, whose opposites inside
had by then birthed others.

No doubt too much division
can turn malignant and spread,
and it's pointless to appeal
for what can't be prevented,

except that it gives me
something like hope
if I pray a thing
can become more alive
each time it splits again in two.

NOBODY KNOWS THEY'RE HERE

In 1995, doctors reported that it is
possible many people are actually twins
walking around in a single body, a phenomenon
they remain oblivious to all their lives.

No wonder, this disaffection with anyone
different from ourselves.
Imagine the beginning:
two mirror images in the womb,
every need met without effort
and the rest of the world
elsewhere in the muffled beyond,

an existence so complete,
who among us wouldn't panic,
conceal the twin inside our body,
be born secretly doubled and doubtful
of the possibilities of other-love?

Not that we don't keep trying.
This man and I, for instance,
two bodies in bed, trying to make up
for two absences, so even at its best
sex is a detour around what both of us
have forgotten has disappeared.

Outside our window
a screech owl arrives feet first
on the back of a rabbit. Small beings
disappear like that a dozen times a day.
Survival of the fittest, we agree,

just before the discontent
begins again, before what's missing
intrudes and I start to catalogue
what I don't like about his odors
and good humor, the way
even our happiness can feel wrong.

THE FIRST SUPPER

Maybe more than a fantasy, the way
I imagined my sister and I started out
not just twins,

but triplets in the womb
like Adam and Eve and an apple,

the two of us breaking
your body between us.

For years, my sister
thought the boogeyman
lived in dresser drawers,

therefore kept them shut,
checked the attic every night,

burned three nightlights
on her side of the room.

The goodnights she insisted upon
never included you.
She whispered not only our names

as her hand clenched mine
across the aisle between our beds,

but the street we lived on,
town, country, planet,

an incantation that took
almost twenty minutes to complete,
as if her need to define our place

were as strong as mine to disappear.
Years later, she tends the sick
and adopts stray cats

while I sidle into a seclusion
I've needed all my life,

as if only there
it might be possible to hear
what you would have said

if we hadn't divvied up
your flesh and blood
and split your tongue between us.

THE SURVIVING TWIN

The past is never dead—it's not even past.
—William Faulkner

When Elvis croons, *Love me tender,*
love me true, he sounds like half of one
missing the other
who might be watching offstage
as silent and still
as the day they were born,
whose thin hips
he must have rolled against
for so many months in the womb.

At midlife a woman with a twin dead at birth
still divides her supper in two,
every meal an eating and not-eating,
and later sees herself
in the middle of a room
from her orbit outside the window,

the way I, under a mirrored ceiling with a lover,
feel as cooly at home
in the eyes that follow
my long-limbed body
as I do in the flesh
that curls and lifts
and carries on without me.

At the edge of everything I do,
one self circles,

The Singer's Temple

changing the tides
of the other one's face,
neither of us ever sure
where the distress calls originate,
which of the two of us
is the uninhabited half.

On hearing his daughter try to play
Offenbach's *Tales of Hoffman*

She's at the piano upstairs,
mangling chords and botching rhythms,
after which he knows she'll rise and curtsy
to applause in an empty living room.

In the office below, his architect's fingers
summon the sonatas abandoned years ago
for something certain and more concrete
and begin to press through the drafting table
to the memory of a Steinway below.

His hands undo her errors,
thumb crossing gracefully under
the second finger, both hands firm
on the chords as he hears the music's
swell of want and illusion.
Even here, surrounded by plans and elevations,
his fingers hunger for remembered keys,
felt-covered hammers striking
the stringed world of vibration and pause
where Hoffman's bride, delicate and gifted,
has been warned that singing would kill her,
and it does, her joy so irrepressible
what could she do but break
into song, collapse in her father's arms?

My brother, who's known the piece since childhood,
plays its final, silent chords
and goes upstairs where his daughter
is twirling on the piano stool, braids flying,
the music book open on her lap.

She's flipping through pages,
wants him to find her something
less difficult to play,
and he, looping her braids on top of her head,
tries to measure the inheritable price
of his refusal.

Wendy Addresses the Women's Group
on the Subject of
Peter Pan and Lost Shadows

In the end, I was the one who knew
that using a bar of soap
to stick his own shadow back on
is something only a small boy would try,

which is what Peter had been doing,
sitting cross-legged on the floor by my bed,
wiping soap and whining
about feeling unattached.

In those nights between losing it
and finding it again, even the Lost Boys complained
that every story he told them sounded evangelical,
full of self-righteous rescues,

that he acted suddenly invincible
and obsessed with keeping his slippers clean.
Had he been old enough to shave, they griped to me,
he would've been at it twice a day
trying to keep the hairiness off.

I can't say whether Peter's shadow plotted
while it waited those nights in the dresser drawer
after my mother yanked it
from the slobbering mouth of Nana the dog,
who'd loved it like a piece of charred meat,

but I told Peter this: living with one's shadow
has more to do with candor than clean living.
And when I rescued his and sewed
it back on his feet I knew,

as Achilles' mother did not,
dipping her son by his heels in the River Styx,
that the unguarded seam between shadow and self
is what every Paris aims for

and most women too, which is what
I believed until I saw the shadow
of the savior in me dismayed
by Peter's restoration and banished him
back to Never-Never Land.

Barbara Hurd   13

NEGATIVE CAPABILITY

The surviving Siamese twin
first reported difficulty with her heart
feeling too confined within one chest.
Sometimes it pressed against scars,
and once, catching sight of herself
in a K-Mart window, she felt pink edges
almost pull apart, as if what's inside
can't forget and dreams of leaping
through sewn doors, back to the mirrored
face, four arms intertwined, to the time
of communal blood. A psychiatrist
called it hysteria, prescribed thorazine,
told her to hang self-portraits all over her house.

She tried an art class where she learned
to refocus, to draw the white space
between posts of a railing, the emptiness
that might define what's there.
She went from art to photographic reversals
for which she posed in a white-walled room.
Inside the red haze of the darkroom light,
a phantom face emerged. She stopped
using "we," then put away smock tops,
found a lover who learned to take her
from behind and never to count on
the part of her body
where the other once lived.

AFTER LISTENING
TO THE SURVIVING SIAMESE TWIN

I take a wide band of cloth
and join my lover at neck and chest,
spend the evening twisted over his shoulder,
him over mine, both of us trying to read.

Later, leaning sideways over the sink,
our mouths full of Crest,
I imagine Eng and Chang
and their two wives, unable
to turn their backs, together
on top, together beneath,

and then I make my lover leave
so I can see how it feels to wake alone
after nights of making love,
the candles blown out,
blankets tucked under my chin.

I'm trying to name the absence
where the other I never had was cut away
and find a reason why my invisible scar
continues to nuzzle any chest within reach,
why I search for men whose every whispered
come here, come closer,
is followed by *go away.*

Barbara Hurd   15

THE DOUBLE LIFE OF VERONIQUE

(from the film of the same name
by Krzyfztof Kieslowski)

1

Though I've never been far from Paris,
I know the worn counter
of the watchmaker's shop in Krakow,
the sweetness of fruited piernik.
All my life I've felt
I was in two places at once.
When I tell my father
I'm never alone
he smiles, says *of course not*,
has no idea what I mean.
Neither do I.
All my life I've been in love
with what I've never met,
surprised over and over
by the inexplicable joy
that comes from making room
in my body for someone else,
by the relief of not feeling obliged
to see the beloved as other.
Lying in bed I hear the deep alto
of a woman two women a woman
singing *Kyrie eleison*—
Lord, have mercy.
I fill a vase with deep blue
buds of closed gentians.

2

I'm walking in a park one night.
An old man strolls by, opens
his coat, and walks on.
I lean against a tree and the moon
yanks back the tides along every coast.
I hear my footsteps on cobblestones,
a loose can against curb.

Along miles of suddenly exposed sand
seaweed lies limp and littered
with fragments of shells.
I stay in bed for days.
I tell my father, who lives alone
in a villa outside of town,
that someone I may not have known
has disappeared from my life.
He is old and loves me
and he tries to understand.
He tells me he remembers
loving a woman,
how for years nothing else mattered
but to wake in her arms.
He cannot remember
who she was or what happened to her.
For years he has had no place to put
what pours out of him still
like water into the desert.
Like that? he asks.

~

Barbara Hurd   17

3

I search for small things
to contain my grief:
violets, doll china,
pocket mirrors I fog
with my breath. A puppeteer
sets up stage in town. He unpacks
a marionnette with my dark hair,
the lead alto in a church choir.
He tells me my name is from
vera-icon, meaning true likeness,
that when Christ handed back
to the woman a handkerchief
he'd used to wipe his brow,
it bore a perfect likeness of his face.
He unpacks a second marionette,
lays her on her side,
head on stage floor, a double,
in case the first one disappears.

LONG-TERM PREGNANCY

One origin is clear—
a night in Dayton, Ohio,
on a pull-out couch visiting
friends at Christmas.

But how to explain
the relief I feel,
finally being—so obviously—
two people at once?

Maybe now it's nighttime.
I might be on my side,
lying still, hands on my belly,
while the life inside rolls over,
presses fingers into mine.

Sometimes my breasts
seem to turn inside out, nipples dangling
inside my body.
Something has pulled
the plum-laden branches
down within reach.

I feel the same relief I imagine
the disciples did when footsteps
approaching on the water
turned out to be God's.

I dream of bolt-locking
the uterine door,

Barbara Hurd   19

wonder how long
the florist will stand
knocking outside
with his arms full of roses.

What Precedes

Monet sees that moment when sunrise
fuses indigo buntings and their song
into a melody of molten blue.

Each brushstroke a note,
he paints the split-second
between sight and recognition—

spangled sails of cathedral walls,
flesh-waves breaking
on a woman's cheek,

pillars of mist steadying
the Amsterdam Bridge.

He is trying to show us
what there is
before we lurch, dripping,
from the tidal-surf,
shaking the wet from our bones.

He paints what precedes,
the world before it's transfixed,
its willingness to spill
one thing into the next,

as if to the gasp of color and light
the only possible response.
is his kind of music.

Barbara Hurd   21

The Singer's Temple

TWO

My twin, the nameless one,
wild in the woods.

—John Berryman

Communion with the Sky Double

*—The Yoruba believe each of us has a sky double,
a being whose actions on a spiritual plane
reflect ours on the earthly plane.*

Without one, I'm body-bound
to the literal, less able to see
the choices I've made
to live in this world without theory.

I like to think of mine as spacious,
a cirrus cloud above the garden
asking me to take off my gloves,
drop to my knees, look up into the firmament
of foxglove blossoms where stars bloom
against the curved sky inside.

It provides me with a way
to refuse what I refuse all
the decarnated gods—
the permission *to take, eat,
this is my body.*

Lonely metaphor of everything I do,
it continues to press me with gifts,
to offer solace, spirit and the chance
which I can't quite accept
that I might matter
more than I do.

If These Two Could Simply Have Dreamed

Leonor Fini's *Red Vision* is a painting
of a conventional room—walls, doorways—
and, hovering on the ceiling, a burning bush

that looks as if it's trying to become human,
twigs fleshing into thighs, a dark eye
squinting from a blotch of claret and peach.

The girl in the center of the room
has removed her shoes
and looked up before the bush was ready.

It raises one finger-flame of caution
to the child, who does not hide her face,
who's on her way to or from being a ghost.

If these two could simply have dreamed
of each other, she could have risen in the morning,
shopped at the market again,
thought herself a poet or painter
obsessed by persimmon flambe.

And whatever's hiding in the bush
could have gone on hiding,
parting the sea, appearing in Blake's window
as a pillar of indigo air.

Instead, I imagine she'll see herself as a doorjamb
straddling a crack of light that might
at any moment burst into flame,

while the other's tongue will thicken with shyness.
Where it might have soon grown a body,
a voice to announce *for I so loved the world*,
it will, for eons, manage only locusts and frogs.

Sudden Exposure

That summer night I walked into his bedroom
and saw my father standing there,
Fruit of the Looms around his ankles,
furred cornucopia spilling between his thighs,
I heard the metal teeth close over my own dark
places so that everything after that went in and out
above my neck, including God whom I tested
and failed again and again until the day
my freshman year when Professor Handley asked
if anyone here loved the Lord and Kenny King
with his dark eyes and soft black curls stood up
and said *yes* and I rolled my eyes and the bells
in the tower chimed and the phone in the next room
rang and Kenny King stood still loving God
right there in front of us like I'd never seen
anyone do before and since I like Kenny King
and wanted to consider exactly what he'd said,
I ran down the list of love and God words—
Adoring the Deity, fancying the Father, having it bad
for the Buddha—but since I had it bad
for not feeling anything I didn't know what he meant
or how even to be friends anymore with someone
who walked all over campus loving God like that
or what to do with sudden fear, this dread
of exposure, never knowing where to look
or how to keep from looking *right there*
where all that dark abundance swirls.

Barbara Hurd

To the Grackle Who
Fell Down the Stovepipe
in a Blizzard

I keep seeing a bird flying blinded
in what used to be sky
where it could see nothing,
not even the black arc
of its own wing.

When it felt that sudden pillar
of warm air rising through nothingness,
it must have hesitated, twisted
its thin neck and looked with one eye
down towards the black circle opening
like a tunnel beneath it.

What will never be known
is whether it tried turning back,
cinders flying up
as its body plummeted,
the way any of us halfway down
a longing far larger than our lives
might try turning back
before the outlines of things
burn beyond recognition.

When it dropped into a bed
of ruby coals, wings beating
wildly against sooted doors,
did it long for the numbness
of blizzards left behind

or do in its bird brain
what I've sometimes done:
insist a too-fully-granted wish
was simply the first half of what I wanted?

CAVING WITHOUT THE SHAMAN

I gathered squirming adolescents around me,
their bodies like uncanned worms,
and reminded them of myths,
how Muhammed heard God's voice in the cave.
I wanted them to write about how it feels
down there, why caves so often symbolize
rebirth. The boys jostled for position,
wanted to be next to the girl
whose blouse was slightly see-through.

We put on overalls, hard hats with lights,
used ropes to drop into a muddy mouth.
While I moved through dim tree roots,
fingered the underbelly of bedrock,
they squealed, turned off their lamps
and felt each other up.

At a tunnel beyond the first underground room,
we followed the leader, lay down on our backs
and wiggled through a chute toward blackness,
where eyeless salamanders spend their lives mouthing
dark interiors and you cannot tell whose cold breath
is whose, I strained my eyes for anything. What I felt

is what my cousin saw,
the Mack truck
bearing down
in his side view mirror
seconds before he died
and the message

on the glass:
Objects in this mirror are closer than they appear.

The membrane stretched too thin, my body
a tangle of fur and fear feels not rope nor light
only the crescendo of wild heartbeat against the wall
and claws its way out seeping tunnels,
gouging fingerholds into mud like wet skin.

Back in bright sunlight I lean against the oak,
mesmerized by tongues and teeth,
how they chatter, bite off bits of bologna sandwiches,
grin. They offer me kool-aid and potato chips.
I shake my head and cannot tell them
what I haven't yet learned
about fasting and rebirth,
how I'm afraid whatever is inside me now
might circle around in here forever.

Barbara Hurd   31

The Question of Dr. Jekyll and Mr. Hyde

A teacher at the chalkboard turns
and imagines pushing desks
together, lowering her body
onto the one whose question
about character and conflict
still lingers in his mouth.

Behind a curtain of textbook and chalk,
she shudders thick and shaded
inside Jekyll's bones, spine twisting in the hands
of what she thought she'd turned to ash
by the heat of her good intentions.

She unbuttons the hugeness of his coat,
hears her voice gone dwarfish and husky,
feels Jekyll's nausea in her mouth,
Hyde's lust grinding in her molars
while stage crews haul away bridges,
drag in back alleys
and the curtain begins to rise.

It's moments like this,
the director gone for coffee,
stage crew caught with their arms full,
when we know what rises in us
is unbidden.

FIREFLIES

Embarrassing, what I noticed
the summer my marriage dissolved:
the male firefly pulsing in flight
while she, wingless, crawls up a grass blade,
tilts her lantern-belly up,
and signals him to her, glow upon glow.

No wonder we gave up, a mindful man
with a woman who wished
we could've stayed luminescent like that,
summoned with flares whatever we longed for,
could've bargained a bit before the mind
pre-empted the light, drew it in,
left us opaque on the outside.

Some day I'll tell him
what I've learned since then
about romance and ambition
as the mind's attempt to disguise
what the body has lost,
just two more well-lit pursuits
in a dark-mattered world.

GREEN SEA URCHIN

Seagreen and trimmed in pearls,
its shell lies cock-eyed on a tidal boulder,
a duplicate of the color photo
in *Peterson's Guide*, Plate 62.

I used to be embarrassed
by easy identification, my own crises
too recognizable—page 43
of Sheehy's *Passages* or Chapter 10 of
Why We Can't All be Artists.

I'd wanted my griefs uniquely mine,
the consolation friends offered
tailored to my particular angst,
and not this field guide matching
of shell-shape and hue.

There's no sign of the globular body,
gulped down, most likely,
by gull or wet-footed fox,
its footprints, too, erased
by the coastline's reminder

that loss, in the end, is mostly about
what happens next, the high tide's
twice daily ritual of wash and retrieve,
right on schedule,
re-arranging the wrackline.

MOLTING

The vacuum cleaner salesman says
eighty percent of household dust
is human skin. He pushes
the nozzle of the latest model
into crevices of my ten-year-old

couch, graveyard of stale popcorn,
lost pens, bits of dog food
the mice have dragged around.
But mostly human skin, he says,
and mattresses are the worst,

sex like a high-speed sander
on all that flesh. It makes him
wonder why we don't do this
more efficiently, maybe shed skin
for a week once a year.

I imagine it hanging in tatters,
barely-visible skull gleaming
like a sacred urn turned
upside down as crumb-litters of skin

cascade down airiness of backbones,
across bony petals of ribs.
He holds his sample vacuum
cleaner bag, full now of the flaked-
off skin of friends, and looks around
for a trash can.

Had I known back then
the shagginess of our bodies,

how differently I might have understood
my own gestures after loss.

If eighty percent of what remains
as thin film on a back corner table
might be the skin of one who's gone,
no wonder the delicacy of my finger
doodling in the dust.

THREE

There is within us only that dark, divine animal
engaged in a strange journey—
that creature who, at midnight, knows its
own ghostliness and senses its far road.
—Loren Eiseley

THE DOGS OF JODHPUR, INDIA

You see them weaving
between the wheels and hooves
of Jodhpur streets,
sleek heads like unopened umber tulips,
skeletons with a film of flesh

or loping out along the paved edge
of acres of ochre sand
where some notion of curiosity or survival
—what, in the end, is the difference?—
drives them over the dunes
out of the sheer sureness
this world's to be swallowed and smelled.

This picture has nothing to do
with pity or guilt
but with asking what we mean
when we say
someone has *gone to the dogs*.
It has to do with rethinking
whether *ruined* might also mean
stripped of the distractions
of hope or a past.

If they think about anything at all
at night, curled again in the doorways
of closed shops, it isn't about betrayal,

someone's decision they're too big
or bark too much,
a bother to keep around the house.

Nobody has ever promised them a thing.

CREATING A COURTYARD DESIGN
IN TAMIL NADU

It's as if she reaches into the world
of what we both know is missing
and brings back handfuls of what rustles there,
lets rice powder fall through fingers and thumb.

Behind her, the walls of her house
look luminescent, the skin of a winter moon
pinned on either side of the doorway,
which is draped, as she is.

Every morning before hauling water,
gathering wood, she kneels in the courtyard,
extends her arm. I watch her fingers
skim the hardened earth,
swirl loose grains of lilac and gold

into heart-shaped petals she hems in white,
filigrees with tendrils and lotus blossoms bronzed
by her belief this ritual will summon the gods back.

Within hours she will bend again in irrigated fields,
pat mud into dams, press seed into furrows
while I wait in the courtyard, blurred now
into puddles and scuffs,
her design dismantled by rain and feet
and the small beaks of birds.

When the Other Teacher is a Goat

Here, after betrayal
in the Blue City of Jodhpur,
one teacher is a woman,
the other a goat.
The woman opens a gate,
offers me apricots, melons, a peach.
The goat's a ruminant wandering the alleys,
his beard-wisp waggling as he chews.
On the wall behind them
is a message in Hindi.
All the letters hang from the upper line
like nooses or chimes.

Hurt's the worst time to choose
between comfort and wisdom.
The satisfying sureness of being
the one so clearly wronged
solicits fresh fruit, a respite,
sympathy the color of the sun.

But India's ashes and endless chants,
its tedium of rebirth, remind me
I've done it that way before,
allowed my feet to be rubbed,
my fresh fruit peeled.
I've even hoped the betrayer
was peering in the window,
watching others offer solace.

She smiles, her sari swaying from her hips;
he gobbles laundry and tin cups
and reminds me of the Buddhist story:

when the last demon wouldn't leave,
the master declared it his teacher
and put his head in its mouth.

PAINTED DOG AT PONGAL FESTIVAL

*(India Festival of the Harvest when the
horns of sacred cows are painted red and yellow)*

In this land where Vishnu
becomes Krishna becomes Rama,
who knows whether this dog appeared
as dog or cow to a drunken man
with a bucket of paint?

Or as a woman in white silk
to an ecstatic priest who blessed her head
with a smear of sandalwood?
Hindus say the world blazes with a divinity
that tinges the skin with crimson
and leaps through human touch.

Scrawny and flea-scarred, ears still airborne,
this dog looks like she's just landed here,
forehead primed with neon pink,
a devotee, a cow.
Whichever, she says,
seated on a painted prayer,
one eye in the sun and one in the shade,
love me, pet me.

RESTRAINT

If I hadn't been on the other side of the globe
with the one who confessed his betrayal,
I would've welcomed meanness,
I would've plotted and delivered,
felt the flourish of the wronged
and boarded a plane headed back.

Ours was an old story stopped this time
by five weeks, six cities, a hundred
thousand rupees yet to go,
and the loneliness we'd each created
and couldn't bear to deepen
this many miles from home.

The temple bells at Eklingi
clang again against my bones.
I'm dangled and swung
between the urge to strike back
and the tale we often tell
about what we still need
that matters more than what's gone.

A village priest presses
his finger to my forehead
and offers me blessings
in exchange for coins and marigolds,
but I'm not consoled.
I'm imagining my lover's head
as the clapper inside a bell,
which strikes me now
as simply a slightly better version
of the old story once again.

Shaving of the Head

If their mothers, wanting them safe, had been Greek,
they might have held these girls by their heels,
lowered them into the River Styx,
prayed for a blessing of protection.

But they are Hindu, outside a temple
where their hair has been shaved and offered to the gods,
their baldness anointed with sandalwood.

They look as if they've been dipped into a river of pollen,
heads seeded with a promise of profusion,
acres of ginger and red chili, a thousand shrines
to a panoply of many-armed gods and goddesses,
all of India's spirit and hunger,
beauty and grime.

This is what they mean by blessing,
though there's nothing said
about being invincible
or if excess can be a kind of armor.

Motorcycle Riding with a Sadhu

The answer we need now will be found if we allow ourself to
be led through the small door of the improbable.
—*A Guide to the I Ching*

No mountain in sight,
no harbor, nothing
that requires the tunnel ahead,

its faint mouth the exact shape
and size of our bodies, nothing
that needs a drilled passage

except this densing I do
in moments of despair,
this brittle compulsion

to be certain of something.
Squeezing the clutch, shifting up,
you know without asking

my urge to harden dunes
to cement, camels to bronze.
You are an auger

I'm trying to ride through substance
toward a small door
that might or might not open.

There's no other map,
you remind me,
than this rift of tremble and veil,

Barbara Hurd   45

no other toll
than a willingness to subside,
which is exactly the improbable

I can't imagine doing
without a plotted, willful act
of my own.

TEMPLE PRIESTESS WITH A GIFT

She only appears when hurt
has made you human again,
though you mustn't think
what she extends is consolation
or forgiveness.

Remember Alice? One bite
makes you small.

She's pointing out a door
you can't go through
without more offerings of your own.

She'll take your clothes, your calendar,
whatever will leave you
embarrassed and adrift.

You may not know for months
she's attached a threshold
to your shoes,

just that footsteps echo
in a chamber without a floor.

Blame means nothing here,
nor does the wish to be elsewhere.
She's set an alarm clock
you can't shut off without
a failure of your own.

FOUR

*Only in the double kingdom, there
alone, will voices become
undying and tender.*

—Rilke (tr. by Robert Bly)

LONGING

I've learned at last to wear a sign
for all prospective lovers: caution
this twin suffers severe
post-coital blues. Bring tissues
and bear in mind it has nothing
to do with you. It's just
the way our faces
resume their shapes,
how those limbs become
your own again
and these, mine; the sudden chill
of sweat on the belly. And then

the memory of intimacy
before birth
when bodies of half-
formed brains and sightless
eyes rolled over one
another for months and
months in a silent watery
world, stubby fingers inter-
twined, knowing nothing
but another
presence in the dark.

The Singer's Temple

SURETY

Wanting a man she's not sure she wants,
a woman climbs up a cliff
and into a cave which hands her
oils: coal-black, cinder-gray, sepia.
Think of it this way, it tells her,
these brushstrokes up his thigh.
It insists she paint and she does,
making the cave's outline
visible under the mountain,
its edges fluted with dripping water.
It wants to see itself
like a mouth turned inside out.
Put the mountain inside me, it says
and she practices with her pockets,
turns them wrong side out, slits open the seams.
The cave wants to leave the country, catch a cab,
walk down a city street, linger in a lingerie shop,
hold a white camisole up to its shoulders.
The cave wants fingers, it wants to twirl a straw,
smash moths against a window.
The woman's sure they should start
by unbuttoning the black silk shirt
of a man who knows how to tremble,
which makes the cave remember
the earthquake of its birth.
They're walking down Market Street toward
the Liberty Bell. Inside it, another cave,
the cave explains, and a clapper swathed in silence.
Let freedom ring the cave starts to sing
but the woman is hungry, wants roast beef,
maybe the man unzipping her dress.

~

Barbara Hurd   51

It wants to dance, it wants hooped earrings, a pierced navel,
a tatoo in the shape of itself on the back of its neck,
something else for the woman to enter on all fours.
It wants to be a funnel, and *you*, it says to the woman, *you*
stand with your mouth open beneath me.
Open wider, it says and they're kissing on the street,
the kind of wide-mouthed kissing
that lets whole stories move back and forth—
betrayal and loss, the debris of our lies,
the memory of a girl who keeps swimming out to sea—
until the cave itself wants to enter the woman,
snaggle its stalactites in her hair
but she's thinking about the man again,
whether she wants to be sipping wine with him
or offering him her breast,
but what to do with this cave, impatient now,
with the partially unbraided, the merely untied shoe.
If he were here, it says to her,
I'd say to him, okay, you too,
and so he's here and the zipper's easy, buttons smooth.
The cave supplies music, an opera singer, an oboe,
it wants their mouths on all its hollow drippings,
no end to this turning inside out.
They crawl out of bed in a high-rise hotel,
two of them shy in the aftermath.
How about religion? it sings, *let's make me a god*
but the woman's sure now that she wants
the cave back in the cliff, that she wants to sleep
with the man in the fissures, under low ceilings,
she wants it all bearing down on them,
dank air and emptiness,
the way they are when they're unsure,
inept, pointed stones beneath their backs,
the batteries in their headlamps gone.

The Singer's Temple

ONE HERE, ONE THERE

You stop at the edge
of wind-swept cedar
and frozen fields

to show me someone
inside you—
a man far out on the ice,

hunkered on a paint bucket,
line dropped through a hole,
fish in the black world

beneath. That night
we waltz by firelight,
naked backs like polished patina

swirling and dipping
in the upstairs room
of a lakeside country inn.

All night
it snows. All night
I think of those fish

and what lures them
from above: snippet of bait,
watery circle of light,

what might happen if this time
I am lifted
through the moon.

Barbara Hurd

At the Manger

After hours on back roads between
wheat-stubbled fields
and ramshackled sheds

we go home to hot bread
and corn chowder,
pile oak on the fire
and lie down, fingers intertwined.

History, especially for us,
meeting now after so many
years, becomes not a weight,

but a forest in December
where the smell of our fire
makes the old animals
lift their heads
and turn to the wind.

Later we lie for long hours
listening to flames shift charred logs
into embers

as love, after all this time,
becomes not just love,
but melancholy too.

Then the animals
rise stiffly to their feet
and inch closer, longing
to lay their large heads
down in our laps.

TWINLEAF

*(of the barberry family: low flowers
of early spring)*

I discovered at an early age
that too much noise and light
signal a split-up,
that closeness with no cover
withers into separate beds.

The twinleaf, for example,
its frond so deeply double-lobed
it resembles the Siamese,
lives only in deep shade,
sacrificing bright bloom
for two leaf-islands joined
by an isthmus of green.

In the woods I love monkshood
and the mouths of closed gentian;
at home, the most inaudible
gestures of love:
your hand in my hair,
marked pages in a book,
three stones on the counter
that signal the night.

When experts warn us
not to keep secrets,
I fret about sun on my head,
what wilts in the blaze.
Let's close the curtains, love,

paint the walls green.
I want us to curl
in the shade of our silence,
our mouths to close
around each other's body

the way my twin and I did
in the prenatal x-ray of the womb:
belly to belly,
our thumbs, like stubby roots,
in one another's mouths.

The Singer's Temple

INCOMPLETION

In labor for millenia, the gods
finally severed each one of us in two
so that on the sixth day
when humans appeared,
it wasn't coolness on damp skin
that made us blink at the eager,
extended hands of strangers,
but a sudden sense of incompletion,
what we understand now
as our first lesson in loss.

It's been like that ever since,
all of us allemanding through the gym,
skipping and moving down the line
of others skipping and moving down the line,
some of us wanting just once
to smell our own sweat or feel our own skin
on the palm stretched toward us.

If, from this wish, we have resented
the usual differences
in body shapes and moods,
our varying degrees of need,
then has come
the most difficult lesson—

that a bond between two humans
requires not just all that we have
but sometimes less,

Barbara Hurd

the unused part of us
lonely, yet reserved
for something other
 than even the best of our loves.

RUSSIAN WATER GRANDFATHER

At midnight, my lover having given up
and left me alone, I put away wine,
warm milk, everything else
that will not do
and crawl into night
with the Russian Water Grandfather
Dyedushka Vodyanoy,
who has dripped into my bedroom
in green robes and reeded cap
chattering and whispering of vile things—
Dyedushka Vodyanoy, who marries limpid girls
without homes and drowns them
when they dare to swim at midnight.

In swamps, in trembling sphagnum beds
I take off my clothes,
wade through waist-high sedges
that hiss against my skin,
hungry for gooseberries,
wild carrots and swamp rose,
anything growing here
where there is no such thing as ground.

My foot, squishing through slime,
moves back as if thirty years
to something once soft and lively,
and I keep my eyes on tamarack trees,
drop to my knees in algae,
thrust hands down into muck,

Barbara Hurd

feel the insides of a child's mouth,
knuckles of her fist.

My arm disappears in wet green earth,
wrist gone, elbow gone, shoulder,
until deep in the mire my fingers curl
around something small and still pulsing
and there on my knees with Vodyanoy,
I rock in the ooze
while deep in the mud
I cup my hands
and everywhere around me
wild water lilies float blossoms,
their long roots suspended.

The Singer's Temple

GREAT EGRET

What sustains it
    it obtains by rotating patience
        with violence, bending its knee

backwards, lowering its leg into water
    like a barefoot ballerina
        in a basin full of mirrors.

Its yellow beak splinters the surface
    the way the horntip of a dream
        will sometimes break

through, jerk you upright in bed
    impale you at the center
        of a fountain of glass.

The mystics say when you finally
    turn your face to the world
        the world will, at last,

show its face to you,
    the way this bird
        and its rippling, wet-feathered version

rupture the membrane
    between them, offer themselves
        to each other as sustenance.

Barbara Hurd   61

DOUBTING THOMAS

Thomas, one of the twelve, called The Twin.
                                    —John 20:24

Seduced by memory no woman
could ever fill, Thomas roamed

crowded streets searching for the shape
of his own head, the familiar lift

of the eyebrow, as if hoping his face
like a mirror could coax his twin

to come home, to see their separate
bodies as illusion, fragments

of a water jar, wet stain sinking again
and again into the sands of Galilee

until, with the past and future
like magnets, the present

in his body thinned beyond slivers,
he dropped it all to follow

the flesh and blood of Christ,
which also disappeared.

Of course he's the one to doubt,
to shrug when others come

full of visions of a resurrected Christ.
And when Christ blesses those who believe

in what they cannot see,
Thomas wants his fingers

on the imprint of those nails,
his hand inside the wound,

as if this crawling into the body
of what is gone

is how we may endure the enormity
of what may some day reappear.

LET THERE BE PEACE

The trick would be to say the name aloud
before the thing exists
and not to mind that no one hears or even sees,
the way a god might have done
before he'd thought of ears or potato eyes
watching what goes on beneath a garden
which he hadn't yet thought of either,
there being no dirt or even sun
until he said to no one in particular,
Let there be light.

Perhaps whatever is unformed
needs a certain sound, like *light*
said over and over,
the way shavings need a magnet,
millions of flinders of glisten
flying toward the sound in his sacred mouth
until the word became clear
and the light was separated from the dark
and evening and morning, the first day.

It might be what Gyuoto monks are doing,
hands folded over bellies from which their breath
goes out into the world. Perhaps they are chanting,
Let there be peace. And peace,
more difficult than light,
might need more than a word and more than a god,
might need centuries of quiet minds,
vibrations of alto and bass in ceaseless hum
over the face of the deep,

choreography of tongue and mouth
helping the rest of the body
from what is
to what could be
and morning and evening, the eighth day.

THE SINGER'S TEMPLE

Where two roads intersected, the ancient Greeks
built temples so travelers could rest
and think about direction.

Within us where even more
than two roads cross,
there's not even a stoplight,
nothing to prevent a collision.

But with every convergence
voices begin
to rise inside a temple.

About the Book

The type and layout of *The Singer's Temple* were designed and composed by Bertha Rogers, using Adobe PageMaker 7.0. The typeface throughout is Transitional 521 Book Type. The book was printed on 60-lb. offset, acid-free, recycled paper in the United States of America by the Courier Printing Corp., Deposit, NY. This first edition is limited to copies in paper wrappers.

About the Author

Barbara Hurd is the author of *Stirring the Mud: On Swamps, Bogs, and Human Imagination* (Beacon 2001), a Los Angeles Times Best Book of 2001, *Objects in the Mirror* (Artscape 1994), and *Entering the Stone: On Caves and Feeling Through the Dark* (Houghton Mifflin 2003). Her essays and poems have appeared in numerous journals, including *Best American Essays 1999, Best American Essays 2001, The Yale Review, The Georgia Review, Orion, Nimrod, Prairie Schooner, New Letters, Audubon, Painted Bride Quarterly, Heliotrope*, and others. The recipient of a 2002 NEA fellowship, four Maryland Individual Artist Awards for Poetry, winner of the Sierra Club's National Nature Writing Award, and finalist for the Annie Dillard Award for Creative Nonfiction and the PEN/ Jerard Award, she is the Wilson H. Elkins Professor at Frostburg State University in Frostburg, MD, where she teaches creative writing.

OTHER BRIGHT HILL PRESS BOOKS

POETRY & FICTION COLLECTIONS

Possom, Shelby Stephenson (forthcoming)
2002 Poetry Chapbook Award

The Last Best Motif, Naton Leslie (forthcoming)
Second Place, 2002 Poetry Chapbook Award

First Probe to Antarctica, Barry Ballard
2001 Poetry Chapbook Award

Heart, With Piano Wire, Richard Deutch
2000 Poetry Book Award
Chosen by Maurice Kenny

Inspiration Point, Matthew J. Spireng
2000 Poetry Chapbook Award

Every Infant's Blood: New & Selected Poems
Graham Duncan

My Father & Miro & Other Poems, Claudia M. Reder
1999 Poetry Book Award
Chosen by Colette Inez

What Falls Away, Steve Lautermilch
1999 Poetry Chapbook Award

Traveling Through Glass, Beth Copeland Vargo
1998 Poetry Book Award
Chosen by Karen Swenson

Boxes, Lisa Harris
1998 Fiction Chapbook Award

To Fit Your Heart into the Body, Judith Neeld
1997 Poetry Book Award
Chosen by Richard Foerster

Blue Wolves, Regina O'Melveny
1996 Poetry Book Award
Chosen by Michael Waters

Whatever Was Ripe, William Jolliff
1997 Poetry Chapbook Award

Low Country Stories, Lisa Harris
1996 Fiction Chapbook Award

My Own Hundred Doors, Pam Bernard
1995 Poetry Book Award
Chosen by Carol Frost

The Man Who Went Out for Cigarettes, Adrian Blevins
1995 Poetry Chapbook Award

ANTHOLOGIES

On The Watershed:
The Natural World of New York's Catskill Mountain Region
Poetry & Prose by Catskill Student Writers, illus.
Edited by Bertha Rogers

The Second Word Thursdays Anthology
Poetry, fiction, and nonfiction by Word Thursdays authors
Edited by Bertha Rogers

The WTWinter & Summer Workshops for Kids
1998 Anthology, BH Books by and for Kids,
Edited by Bertha Rogers

Out of the Catskills and Just Beyond: Literary and Visual Works by
Catskill Writers and Artists, with a Special Section by Catskill High-
School Writers and Artists,
Edited by Bertha Rogers

Speaking the Words Anthology
Edited by Bertha Rogers,

The Word Thursdays Anthology
Edited by Bertha Rogers

Iroquois Voices, Iroquois Visions
Edited by Bertha Rogers
Contributing editors:
Robert Bensen, Maurice Kenny, Tom Huff

ORDERING BRIGHT HILL PRESS BOOKS

BOOKSTORES: Bright Hill Press books are distributed to the trade by Small Press Distribution, 1814 San Pablo Ave., Berkeley, CA 94702-1624; Baker and Taylor, 44 Kirby Avenue, POB 734, Somerville, NJ 08876-0734; and North Country Books (regional titles), 311 Turner St., POB 217, Utica, NY 13501-1727. Our books may also be found at BarnesandNoble.com and Amazon.com.

INDIVIDUALS: If your local bookstores do not stock Bright Hill Press books, please ask them to special order. Or order directly from us by using the order form below and sending it to: Bright Hill Press, POB 193, Treadwell, NY 13846 or to our e-mail address—wordthur@catskill.net, by fax at 607-829-5056, or by phone at 607-829-5055. We accept MasterCard and VISA, or you may enclose check or money order. Please add $3.50 for the first book and $.75 for each additional book for shipping and handling. (For *Out of the Catskills and Just Beyond*, *The Second Word Thursdays Anthology*, and *On the Watershed* add $3.95 for the first book and $1.75 for each additional book for S&H). There is a 20% discount on orders of 3 or more books. Members receive a 10% discount on all orders.

The Singer's Temple

ORDER FORM
(THIS PAGE MAY BE DUPLICATED)

_____

Title(s)_____

Quantity_____Price(s)_____++_____

Shipping & Handling_____Subtotal_____

SALES ₁AX_____

**NEW YORK STATE RESIDENTS, AND WHERE APPLICABLE
NOTE: We cannot process orders without payment of applicable sales tax.**

(Orders of 3 or more, subtract 20% off total before sales tax)

Member discount (10% off total before sales tax)_____

Shipto_____

CHECK OR MONEY ORDER: AMOUNT ENCLOSED $_____
(includes price of book(s), shipping, and applicable taxes)

MasterCard_____ VISA_____

Card Account Number_____

Card Expiration Date: Month_____Year_____

Customer Signature_____

Card-Issuing Bank Name_____